PAWS
AGAIN

MAUREEN MELVIN
Illustrated by Geoff Crook

CHAPMANS
1991

Also by Maureen Melvin
with illustrations by Geoff Crook

PAWS FOR THOUGHT

Dearest Daddy, never fear,
Let's forget you pruned my ear.
Open up the best champagne;
Here, for you, is *Paws Again*!

Chapmans Publishers Ltd
141-143 Drury Lane
London WC2B 5TB

A CIP catalogue record for this book is available from the British Library

ISBN 1-85592-561-3

First published by Chapmans 1991

Designed by Judy Linard
Typeset by Monoset Typesetters
Printed and bound in Great Britain by
The Bath Press, Avon

Author's Note

When my *Paws for Thought* was published
I believed I'd done my bit,
Written down my thoughts and feelings –
That would be the end of it.

After all the great excitement,
Interviews and radio shows,
Lots of trips by train to London,
Extra chocs and Bonios,

Suddenly, my peace was shattered:
Letters came from far and wide,
Down from Afric's sunny fountains
Up to Scotland's Firth of Clyde.

Cats and dogs of all descriptions,
Grown-up people, children too,
Wrote me poems and picture postcards
Begging me to start anew.

So, I've had to work my tail off,
With the midnight oil in train.
Now, at last, it's done – Hey Presto!
Here I am with *Paws Again*.

What's in a Name?

My name is Abigail of Course.
I've always wondered why
I have no proper surname
Like McGregor, Hunt or Bligh.

I scrutinised my pedigree
To see what it would show.
There's Rosamund of Ottermouth
And Merry Matelot.

There's Gorgeous Girl of Eyeworth
(A lady of the night!),
And Applecourt Delinquent,
But not a Course in sight.

I tried my *Great World Atlas*
To locate my title source.
I found a place called Corsica –
The French pronounce it 'Corse'.

So maybe that's the answer.
Though I'm British through and through,
I'm very keen on Sole Bonne Femme
And Mummy likes it too.

And signing cards for Christmas,
Which I happily endorse,
She writes: 'With love from Him and Her
And Abigail of Course.'

Sunday Papers

I know on Sunday morning,
When you get up rather late,
That something nice will happen
If I only stand and wait.
And when you've had your breakfast
And I've washed my morning face,
Then it's off in the Mercedes
For the Sunday paper chase.

I often drive with Mummy
When she's shopping at the store,
But she's only got a banger,
And it's such a crashing bore
For she crawls along at fifty.
But when I am out with you
We go speeding up the highway
At a steady sixty-two!

I love your big blue motor,
And I think it's really neat
To have electronic windows
And an air-conditioned seat,
And a telephone that talks to you
From somewhere in the air,
And an automatic seat belt
To secure me in my chair.

"... CERTAINLY !... MAY I ASK
WHO'S CALLING ?"...

I like to choose the papers
From the Sunday paper rack,
But I sometimes take too many
And you make me put them back.
We'll hurry home for coffee
And I'll watch the hedgerows pass,
And perhaps I'll see some rabbits
Having breakfast in the grass.

We'll stretch out in the garden,
In a hammock made for two,
I'll commandeer the *Telegraph*
And leave *The Times* for you.
You'll scour the city pages,
Which will wipe away your smile.
I'll focus on Sir Peregrine –
I rather like his style.

I know it drives you wild to see
The papers in a mess,
So I'll try to get the paw marks
Off the back of the *Express*.
And when they're all in order
And we've read the whole darn bunch,
I'll stroll into the kitchen
And inspect the Sunday lunch.

Every Silver Lining has a Cloud

I went to stay in London – it was '88, I guess –
At a charming little pad in Eaton Square.
You would think I'd be in clover having such a smart address
But it's not all beer and skittles living there.

There are gardens down the centre of this gilt-edged thoroughfare
Where the residents can stroll about and chat.
And with all those open spaces, there are only two to spare
For the pressing needs of well-trained dog and cat.

We used to go at six a.m. to beat the morning rush,
For the canine population was immense.
And those well-heeled dogs had manners that would make a sailor blush
If he'd seen the things they did behind the fence.

I'd had my vaccination but it wasn't quite enough
To withstand the glut of germs in South-West One.
And when I developed aches and pains and started feeling rough
Then I knew my Waterloo had just begun.

They wrapped me up in blankets on that day I won't forget,
And we drove at breakneck speed down the M4.
By the time we got to Wiltshire and went in to see the vet
Well, I really felt I couldn't take much more.

I had a private room, of course – I'm heavily insured –
And the vet prescribed a pill to make me sleep,
And the last thing I remember was the dog next door, who snored,
Then I crumpled on my sick bed in a heap.

I must have been delirious. I don't remember much
As I drifted through the shadows in a dream.
Then one morning I felt better and my head was cool to touch,
So I rang the bell for strawberries and cream.

The nurses took me out for walks to cure my wobbly legs
And I felt a little stronger every day.
But the best was when they woke me with a plate of scrambled eggs
And the news that I was leaving right away.

I dashed out through reception and I jumped into the car,
For I couldn't wait to get back home again.
They'd prepared my favourite chicken 'cos I don't like caviare,
And they toasted me, all evening, in champagne.

Pointed Glances

There's a tea towel Mummy dotes on in the kitchen,
With almost every dog that you could see.
There are Boxers and Alsatians,
Pomeranians and Dalmatians,
But there's not a single dog that looks like me.

I've aimed some pointed glances at that tea towel,
And I think she's got the message loud and clear,
For with colleagues such as these –
Poodle, Pug and Pekinese –
I'm amazed they've overlooked the Cavalier.

I'll not be too surprised if, come next Christmas,
There's a special parcel waiting on my shelf
With a tea towel which discloses
Abigail in various poses,
Then I won't mind drying dishes by myself!

SPECIAL BRAND

17

Grooming

When my black coat and my white coat turn a nasty shade of grey
And my ears and nails and hair are in a mess,
I can guarantee it won't be long before the dreaded day
When I'm taken to be groomed by Mrs S.

It's the only beauty parlour for discriminating dogs,
And the book she likes her visitors to sign
Is a glowing testimonial from all the local nobs
With a coronet on every other line.

She will greet us with a smile, exchange my collar for a noose,
Then she'll chain me up and hook me into place.
Mummy sidles through the doorway with a rather lame excuse
Leaving me and Mrs Stallard face to face.

'Close your eyes and think of England' is my motto for the day
As I'm clipped, unsnarled, unheeded and unheard.
Then it's splash into the bathtub with the soapsuds and the spray,
To be lathered, laundered, shaken but not stirred.

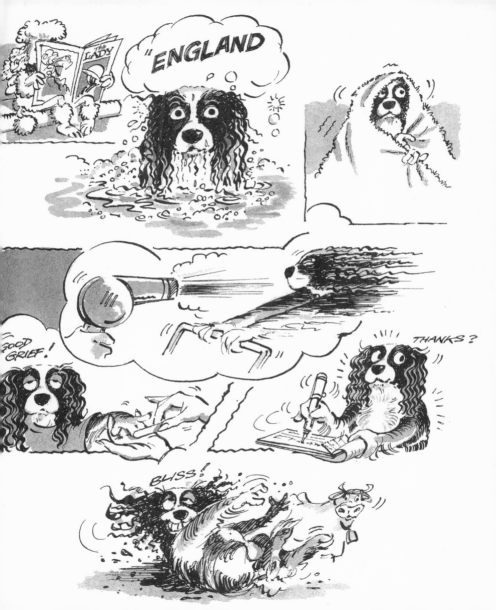

She will wring me out and rub me down and wrap me in a towel,
Then the wind machine starts blowing in my face.
Here's where I exhibit great restraint and moderate my growl,
As the dryer tries to blast me into space.

While she puts the final touches to my whiskers and my toes,
I'll have time to reconnoitre, just to see
If her illustrated apron still conveniently shows
Every kind of dog including one like me.

Now the ordeal's nearly over, and I thank my lucky star
When I hear the motor purring up the drive.
So I pay the bill, express my thanks and leg it to the car
For my favourite TV programme starts at five.

There's a lot of 'Aren't you beautiful' and 'What a pretty girl',
As I settle in the kitchen on my rug.
If they knew what I was planning they'd be really in a whirl
And they wouldn't sit there looking quite so smug.

For at crack of dawn next morning I'll be on my merry way
To have breakfast with the horses while it's hot.
Then I'll pop into the cowshed just to pass the time of day
And I'll finish with a roll in you know what.

Should you happen to regard me as a shameless ne'er-do-well
Be assured I'm used to nothing but the best.
And I'm honoured to be one of Mrs Stallard's clientele
At the finest little salon in the West.

Favourite Food

I'm quick off the mark when it's kippers
Though there's nothing left over for me.
Now if someone would buy me some flippers
I could fish for my own in the sea.

It's great when they're grilled to a cinder
And the heads and the tails topple off.
But the bones are like pieces of tinder
And they sure make you splutter and cough.

I think, in a former existence,
I was quite a fastidious cat,
For I've never shown any resistance
To smoked haddock or mackerel or sprat.

I used to have bones that they bought me,
But they don't buy me bones any more;
It all stopped on the day that they caught me
Digging holes in the dining-room floor.

My red letter day is a Sunday
When it's chicken or beef or roast lamb.
Then it's cold cuts for me on a Monday,
And I might get a slice of smoked ham.

At Christmas it's really quite thrilling
With a turkey that's bigger than me,
Stuffed with chestnut and sausagemeat filling.
But I have to miss afternoon tea.

I suppose I'm a bit of a gourmet,
And of omelettes a great connoisseur,
But I do like my eggs à la mornay
And they're frightfully good for the fur.

It's marrowbone biscuits at daybreak,
And choc-coated ones for my tea,
And my bedtime digestive and milkshake
Is the best sort of nightcap for me.

God bless you, Mouse

There is Something in the cupboard in the corner by the stairs
And it's not as small as butterflies and not as big as bears.
At night it grows adventurous and runs around the house,
And at last I know for certain that the Something is a mouse.

When I was dreaming by the fire of strange and distant lands,
He strolled across the open hearth and paused to warm his hands.
My eyes were standing out on stalks, I quite forgot to chase.
When I pulled myself together he had vanished into space.

And now he comes to visit when the family is in bed.
He curls up on my beanbag and amazing things are said.
He tells me tales of derring-do and breaking out of traps,
And relatives with wooden legs and other small mishaps.

I find that he's a fieldmouse and he leads an active life:
In summertime he lives outdoors and picnics with his wife.
He roams around the countryside engaged on mouse affairs,
But in winter it's the cupboard in the corner by the stairs.

I'm sad to say when people are confronted by a mouse
They often have the vapours or run screaming from the house.
I think they should remember this behaviour may offend.
I like my little fieldmouse and I'm proud to be his friend.

James

I often watch the programme on my television set
Where people find relations that they've never even met.
They fall about, and laugh and cry, they never come to blows.
It isn't always quite like that, I speak as one who knows.

It happened in December, on the day we bought the tree,
That Daddy phoned to say he'd met a Cavalier like me.
He saw him sitting in a car outside a big hotel,
A sleek and snooty London dog, a real Belgravia swell.

29

When Daddy met the owner of this master of the Rolls
She told him James was born in March like all good Pisces souls,
And when they had consulted notes and pedigrees and logs
They found we'd both been bought in May from Town and Country Dogs.

This James, he is a city dog and rides about in cars.
He sleeps all day in offices and drinks all night in bars.
I don't expect he gets a walk except in Eaton Square –
And we know what can happen to a dog who lingers there.

He's trim and clean and well behaved, and slim – and svelte, of course.
I bet he doesn't even know his elbow from a horse;
I don't suppose he's ever met a pheasant or a fox.
Perhaps he gets his kicks from watching wildlife on the box.

30

It's easy to look perfect when you're mincing round the square
With gleaming coat and polished nails and freshly laundered hair.
But James, he is the Town dog and the Country sort is me
And if I had to choose again I know which one I'd be.

I'm sick of hearing 'James does this' and 'James would not do that'
Whenever I've been chasing ducks or fighting with the cat.
I've half a mind to take a train and go to London town,
And give that pompous little prig a proper dressing down.

I'll search him out, and track him down, and beard him in his lair,
And nip him in a tender spot – and I'm not saying where.
And if my plan of sweet revenge goes through without a hitch,
He'll be convinced that he's a dog and certain I'm a bitch!

Haute Couture

If I become a famous dog,
Appearing on TV,
I'll have to wear designer clothes
To make the most of me.

Lounging pyjamas – silk, of course –
When friends drop in for tea,
A morning suit, an evening gown,
And lots of après-ski.

I'll have to hold my tummy in
And diet a little harder
To wear J. H. Collectibles,
Costelloe or Escada.

And when I'm set to cut a dash,
And strolling up and down,
The world will say, 'There's Abigail,
The smartest dog in town!'

Lend Me Your Ear

I know that Daddy loves me –
Of that there is no doubt.
He slips me lots of special treats
When Mummy's not about.

This high regard is mutual;
I was very fond of him
Until the day he went berserk
And gave my ear a trim.

He seized the kitchen scissors
And, somehow, contrived to shear –
By accident and not design –
Three inches off my ear!

Of course, he was beside himself,
And I was quite distraught.
I'm ragged and lopsided
And I'm listing hard to port.

When Mummy saw the damage
She was really in a stew.
I won't reveal the details,
But the air turned rather blue.

She says it won't take long to grow,
I only hope she's right.
I look like Orphan Annie
And I feel a perfect fright.

Next day, when we went shopping
It was more than I could bear,
I caught a Yorkie smirking
And my friends all stopped to stare.

Things haven't been too rosy
With my finest feature docked:
Poor Daddy's on probation
And the scissor drawer is locked.

I've been too vain about my ears,
Too mighty and too high.
'Pride goes before a fall,' they say,
And now I realise why.

Wielding the Willow

I like a game of cricket in the fields or by the sea,
And friends will come from far and wide to play the game with me.
I pick my team at random from whoever seems the best
I'm captain of The Ladies and The Bounder runs The Rest.

The Bounder is a hound I met when he was past his prime,
But rumour has it he was quite a player in his time.
His dignity commands respect from all the junior pack;
His strategy is masterly when planning his attack.

Our regular recruits include two Collies from close by –
Young Laddie who's a sprinter and Old Spot who's not so spry –
Two Labradors from up the lane who often cause a rift.
They have the killer instinct but they give the game a lift.

Now Tink, who hails from Devon, is a Lurcher acrobat,
A dastardly spin bowler and a demon with the bat,
But when she makes a catch she goes on running at full power,
Then swims off round the headland and is gone for half an hour.

Two Dachshunds, Port and Starboard, sail from Guernsey every spring.
They practise at the nets for hours, convinced The Game's The Thing.
They're not much good as batsmen, being stunted in the joint,
But Port is great at deep square leg and Starboard's grand at point.

With Busby, Fred and Charlie Two, all Cairns of high degree,
There's every prospect of a scrap before we break for tea.
But Sapphire, who's a Cavalier and star of stage and screen,
Can always be relied upon to keep the party clean.

Though Oscar is an obstacle, we have to let him play –
A plucky little Yorkie, most appealing in his way.
But while his partner wields the bat he cannot hang about,
He hurtles blindly down the pitch and runs the fellow out.

We find the wickets hidden where we buried them before
And mark the pitch precisely on the firm and sandy shore.
I put The Bounder in to bat, he knows that I'm the boss;
I use my double-headed coin and always win the toss.

I call the shots all afternoon and change the teams halfway.
On sunny days we carry on until bad light stops play.
There tends to be a problem over adding up the score,
It saves a heap of trouble if we finish with a draw.

When stumps are drawn and buried and the sun's about to sink,
We linger in the sand dunes with a sandwich and a drink
Reflecting on the highlights and the finer points of play,
And plans are made to keep in touch and meet another day.

From this athletic spectacle it must be plain to see
It's not the sort of cricket to impress the MCC.
But dogs like us are not concerned with how the game is run.
As Oscar has been heard to say, 'It's just a bit of fun.'

But I have dreams of greatness when I'm sleeping in my bed,
And no one knows the centuries I've made inside my head.
I stroll to the pavilion, and the sporting world applauds
When I retrieve the Ashes for The Ladies up at Lords.

In the Doldrums

Life hasn't been much fun of late,
My plans are up the spout,
'Cos Mummy's *hors de combat*
Since her cartilage conked out.

I took my bone and books and grapes
And sat beside her bed.
She didn't want to read or play,
Just lay and stroked my head.

She said a friend would take me out
But that was only talk.
I haven't had a kipper
And I haven't had a walk.

And when they take the plaster off
We'll still be in a fix:
We can't go chasing rabbits
If she's stomping round on sticks.

But when she's on her feet again,
We'll race along in style.
I'll let her win the 100 yards
And beat her in the mile!

Abigail's Christmas Message

You're going to buy a Christmas dog?
Please pause before you do,
For Christmas is a troubled time
For dogs both old and new.

With all that noisy Christmas cheer
We dogs can feel *de trop*.
Sometimes we don't know what to do
Or even where to go.

We need an airing every hour
Especially when we're small.
We cannot help those little pools
That happen in the hall.

And when we romp around the house
With wet and muddy paws,
We do not mean to tear your tights
Or spoil your parquet floors.

You cannot send us packing
When the going gets too tough.
You cannot fling us from a car
Or lose us in the rough.

Please think before it comes to this
And sunshine turns to strife.
A dog is not a Christmas toy,
A dog is yours for life.

Putting on the Dog

I've never been mad about jewellery
With my figure, my face and my fur –
Just a watch that has stopped
For it's frequently dropped
And a choke chain that wrecks my coiffeur.

But now that my books have been published,
And I mix with the *crème de la crème*,
It would only be right
When out dining at night
To display the odd bauble or gem.

I found a boutique called Gazebo.
Mr Jeffrey presided himself.
They were having a sale,
But it went to my tail
And I swept all the rings off the shelf.

And now I'm attired like a duchess
I shall upstage the long-haired élite.
In my diamond tiara
I'll shine like a star
With the literary world at my feet.

My Valentine

The cards arrived from cats and dogs
And many a long-haired beau.
But one ran circles round the rest –
A purebred Romeo.

A Cavalier King Charles, like me –
Prince Rupert is his name –
Had read my book, which touched his heart,
And lit a white-hot flame.

He wrote a poem and offered me
His matrimonial paw
In terms so complimentary
No girl could ask for more.

How many take a wife on trust
And woo her sight unseen?
Well, that's what Rupert did to me,
And that's what I call keen!

Circumstances, I fear, are such
That I can never wed.
Dear Rupert, try to understand
And be my friend instead.

At Needlepoint

When Mummy does her tapestry
I sit and wait for hours.
I like to watch her stitching scenes
Of birds and bees and flowers.

But sometimes she goes overboard,
It nearly drives me bats.
Her latest *tour de force* involves
A pair of stuck-up cats.

I hurried to the sewing shop
To stake my counterclaim.
I bought some dog-sized needles, wools,
A canvas and a frame.

Now Mummy sits and watches me
Amazed at my design.
My work reveals a famous dog –
An ancestor of mine!

Framed

Many have praised my sparkling eyes
For shape, for colour and for size,
And though I find it hard to write
I've always had fantastic sight.

I read *The Times* and *Daily Mail*,
And crack the crossword without fail.
But nowadays I have to squint
To figure out the smaller print.

When poring over *Horse and Hound*
The letters blur and swim around,
And when the hunt is out in force
I can't distinguish hound from horse.

Out in the fields I sometimes fall
In rabbit holes; but, worst of all,
Rabbits who gave the widest berth
Now double up in tucks of mirth.

And when I turn and start to chase
They thumb their noses in my face,
And scurry off behind a tree
Assuming that I cannot see.

The pros and cons and whys and whens
Of spectacles v. contact lens
Do not apply: in either case
They would not suit my style of face.

There's only one solution here –
It's going to cost a bomb, I fear –
But what a thrill if I could get
Some pearl-encrusted, gold lorgnette.

Taking it on the Chin

Poor Daddy went off to the doctor,
A nasty red rash on his chin.
I thought he'd need antibiotics,
Or ointment for soothing the skin.

He came back, at last, with the verdict.
I sat at his feet, all agog.
He told me the doctor had asked him
What contact he had with his dog.

When Daddy described our relations
As loving and close as could be,
He said I'd have mites in my topcoat
And the cause of the trouble was me!

I begged for a second opinion,
That swift diagnosis to scorn.
But Daddy said, 'Out of the question',
And I wished I had never been born.

So, no more embraces at bedtime;
No curling up small on his knee.
I'm keeping a very low profile
'Cos Daddy's allergic to me!

Second Thoughts

Remember what I said about the Corgi?
I told you they are not as royal as me.
Well, events have taken place
Which corroborate my case
In a way that I would not have wished to see.

One morning, when I gathered up the papers
The news was hot, the worst I'd ever seen.
Big black letters – inches high –
And the thing that caught my eye
Was a headline reading, 'CORGI BITES THE QUEEN!'

I took them back to bed to learn the details
And boned up on the facts for half an hour.
What a horrifying tale –
And I turned distinctly pale
When I thought that dog might end up in the Tower!

We all do things, sometimes, that we're ashamed of.
I snapped at Mummy once; it made her wince.
Well, she jabbed me with her cane
When I dawdled in the lane
And I'm pleased to say she hasn't done it since.

Man leans towards the democratic status;
For dogs, to be supremo is a must.
We enjoy a friend, it's true,
But when faced with more than two,
Then the pecking order tends to bite the dust.

But still, no matter what the provocation,
There are limits to the follies we pursue.
And to bite the hand that feeds,
Just to see if blue blood bleeds,
Is the sort of thing no Cavalier would do.

Dog-Watch

When signing my books in the pet shop at Harrods
A chance in a lifetime occurred.
I was browsing around by the tropical fish
And a rather extraordinary bird –

When I spotted a stack of spectacular watches,
The finest you ever did see.
On each watch was the face of a pedigree dog
And I found one exactly like me.

I carry no money, but Daddy helped out
And he said it could go on his bill.
So the girl wrapped it up in a neat little box
And we settled the deal at the till.

I long to give Mummy this wonderful watch –
She's forever enquiring the time.
And she's always at hand when I'm writing my books,
Which is great when I'm stuck for a rhyme.

I'm keeping it hidden till Christmas comes round
And thank goodness, that's one off my list.
Then she'll have no excuse to be late for my walk
For I'll always be there on her wrist.